# The Power of Influential Leadership

*Skills Proven to Harness the Power of Other People*

☐ **Copyright 2016 by Lifestyle Initiative, Inc.- All rights reserved.**

This document is geared towards providing exact and reliable information in regards to the topic and issue covered. The publication is sold with the idea that the publisher is not required to render accounting, officially permitted, or otherwise, qualified services. If advice is necessary, legal or professional, a practiced individual in the profession should be ordered.

- From a Declaration of Principles which was accepted and approved equally by a Committee of the American Bar Association and a Committee of Publishers and Associations.

In no way is it legal to reproduce, duplicate, or transmit any part of this document in either electronic means or in printed format. Recording of this publication is strictly prohibited and any storage of this document is not allowed unless with written permission from the publisher. All rights reserved.

The information provided herein is stated to be truthful and consistent, in that any liability, in terms of inattention or otherwise, by any usage or abuse of any policies, processes, or directions contained within is the solitary and utter responsibility of the recipient reader. Under no circumstances will any legal responsibility or blame be held against the publisher for any reparation, damages, or monetary loss due to the information herein, either directly or indirectly.

Respective authors own all copyrights not held by the publisher.

The information herein is offered for informational purposes solely, and is universal as so. The presentation of the information is without contract or any type of guarantee assurance.

# Table of Contents

**INTRODUCTION** .................................................................. 5

**CHAPTER 1 – LEARN ABOUT THE PLAYING FIELD** ........................................................................... 7
- TYPES OF POWERS OF LEADERS IN AN ORGANIZATION ............... 8
  - Authoritative power ...................................................... 8
  - Reward power ............................................................. 10
  - Coercive power ........................................................... 11
  - Expert power .............................................................. 13
- WHAT SHOULD THE LEADER DO IN YOUR ORGANIZATION? ....... 14

**CHAPTER 2 – LEARN ABOUT YOUR FOLLOWERS** ................................................................. 21
- WHO ARE YOUR FOLLOWERS? ............................................... 21
- WITH GREAT POWERS COME GREAT RESPONSIBILITIES ............. 24
- WHAT DO YOU WANT YOUR FOLLOWERS TO DO? ..................... 25

**CHAPTER 3 – PUT YOURSELF IN YOUR FOLLOWERS' SHOES** ............................................................................. 28

**CHAPTER 4 – AIM TO MAKE ALL STAKEHOLDERS HAPPY** ............................................................................. 35

**CHAPTER 5 – WORK ON IMPROVING YOUR REPUTATION** ...................................................................... 40

**CHAPTER 6 – SUBTLE TRICKS TO INFLUENCE PEOPLE** ............................................................. 58

**CHAPTER 7 – MOTIVATING FOLLOWERS FOR LONG-TERM TASKS** ................................................ 69

**CONCLUSION** .................................................................. 77

of the organization without ruining your relationships and burning bridges.

Thanks again for downloading this book. I hope you enjoy it!

# Introduction

I want to thank you and congratulate you for downloading the book, *"The Power of Influential Leadership."*

This book contains proven steps and strategies on how to use your influence to maximize the productivity of the people around you.

With the tips in this book, you will be able to build your reputation as an effective leader. You will be able to communicate your message to your followers with authority. You will also be able to build important relationships that will help you do your job better.

This book approaches leadership as a process of dealing with people. With the topics discussed in this book, you will learn how you can maximize engagement from your followers.

You will learn how you can boost their motivation and focus in order to meet short-term and long-term goals. You will be able to push them to work for the goals capabilities, you should first learn what types of powers you have in the organization.

## *Types of powers of leaders in an organization*

### Authoritative power

Authoritative power refers to the type of influence that comes with the position. Sometimes, the mere mention of a position of the person will make a person instantly influential. If you are a CEO of your company for example, you should expect the people of your company to listen every time you speak. If you combine this power with other types of power that will be discussed below, you can become an effective leader.

However, over time, this type of power wanes if you do not back it up with actions. You need to remind people that you have this kind of power every now

# Chapter 1 – Learn About the Playing Field

Being a leader requires you to know everything about the goal of the organization and the tasks required to reach that goal. It requires you to be at your best so that you can push other people to give their best.

What is leadership?

Leadership usually refers to the characteristics of a person in authority. However, in this book, leadership means much more than the position. Leadership means that you have certain types of powers in your organization and you use those powers to influence your followers to reach the organization's goals.

What does leadership mean for your job?

Leadership is a highly complex process that requires you to be aware of the people and the things happening around you. For you to know your leadership

If the person was given the position without working for it, the followers may not respect both.

## Reward power

Sometimes, a certain person gains power based on his or her ability to give rewards. A teacher for example, has this type of power over his or her students because he or she controls the grades of the students.

In the corporate world, this type of power refers to the ability to provide monetary rewards such as bonuses. It could also refer to the ability of a person to influence the organization on who to promote.

You do not have to hold a key leadership position to have this kind of power. If you are in charge of food in meetings for example, you have the power to give extra amounts of food to certain people. If the people in your meeting value what you offer, you have this type of power over them.

and again. You need to remind them why you are in the said position.

Authoritative power only becomes effective when the followers respect both the position and the person holding it. Followers respect the position if past holders of that position are respectable. We instantly respect the president of the country for example, because of the weight of the responsibility and the multiple great men who have held the position in the past. People will also respect the position if it holds a lot of social influence. The police uniform for example, is universally respected symbol by the citizens because of its power to serve and protect.

In most cases, people will only respect the person holding the position if he or she worked for it. If he or she stole it from somebody more deserving of the post, the followers may lack respect for the person holding thee position.

As a leader, you should identify your own reward powers. Rewards are effective in boosting the motivation of your followers, especially the ones at the lowest ranks in the organization.

## Coercive power

This type of power refers to the ability of a person to give punishments. In the most basic unit of society, the family, the parents often have this type of power over their children. The parents can take away privileges from the children and the children needs to respect the parents' wishes if they want to keep the privileges that they are given.

In the public setting, police officers have coercive powers over wrongdoers. If a person breaks the law, the police officers may have the coercive power to detain that person. Everybody fears going to prison so we respect the police when they are present. In cases of emergencies, we follow what they say to avoid their coercive power.

An effective should reflect on what his or her coercive powers are over his or her followers. In most cases, you only need to use this type of power to threaten people. However, in the event that you need to use it, you should be able to walk your talk. You will instantly lose your influence over your followers if they find out that you are only giving empty threats.

**Referent power**

Referent power refers to the power of a person to gain respect based on personal qualities. In some cases, a person just gains respect because of who he or she is. Steve Jobs for example, had this kind of power in Apple in the later part of his career. Regardless of what function he took, people looked up to him and followed his leadership.

This type of power also shows why some teachers in a school are effective leaders while others are not. A teacher that is more charismatic to his students is more likely to gain respect than a teacher who abuses his or her authority.

To have this kind of power, you need to protect your reputation especially among your followers. It is necessary to be trustworthy in the eyes of your followers. You should also avoid activities that may affect your reputation negatively.

**Expert power**

Lastly, you may also gain power for being an expert at your craft. Expert power is the type of power that doctors and lawyers instantly get from their patients or clients. The people relying on these professions follow what the doctor or the lawyers do because of their knowledge in their field.

In most cases, expert power has a direct relationship with the number of years that a person had spent in the industry. A rookie coach for example, should expect to receive less respect than a veteran coach did. In the same way, you will be considered an expert in your industry if you clock in more practice and work experience.

Past successes and achievements also add to your expert power. A coach that has won a championship will be considered better than those without a championship will. You will also be consider an expert in your field if you have a reputation of being a winner or an achiever in your field.

### *What should the leader do in your organization?*

Now that you know what types of power you have over your followers, you should identify what you need to do using those powers. In most cases, you need to use your leadership powers to help the organization achieve its prioritized goals.

A company usually has vision and mission statements to let everybody know about its goals. However, in some cases, the organization's priorities are not related to these statements. It is a leaders' role to identify the true goal of the organization and to help steer its time, energy and resources towards the goal.

As a leader, it is your role to always remember the organizational goals. You need to show your followers your understanding of the goal and that you are focused on it day in and day out.

Let's say you stated that the primary goal of the company is to double the sales numbers from last year. However, you rarely meet your sales team to discuss performance and strategies. You also do more administrative work than sales related activities. As a result, your followers may think that you are not focused on the goal.

In contrast, an effective leader in this situation would set the pace by showing his or her followers how much work he or she is putting in. You should practice this in your leadership roles to show that the goal is your priority. Find a way to show your followers that you are exercising your leadership powers solely for the organization to reach its goal.

## Learn about your industry

Aside from learning about your own skills and the priorities of the organization, effective leaders also learn about the industry where their organization is a part. If you are working for a tech company for instance, learn of the updates in your industry especially about your competition. Also, be aware of economic and political changes that affect your organization's ability to reach its goals. As a leader, you must also take note of the changes in the factors that affect the productivity of your followers.

Effective leaders take advantage of all the free information they can get their hands on. For instance, you could study press materials from within the organization. You will learn a lot about the marketing strategies of your company by studying how it interacts with the press.

Aside from this, you should also be aware of all the memos and other forms of internal communications. Try to look for changes in policies of the company. It is also advantageous to learn about the positions available in the company and the new positions that are being created.

By attending the quarterly meetings for example, you learn a lot about the current state of your organization. You will learn a lot about the organization and the industry by engaging with other leaders and followers.

To be totally aware of the things happening in your industry, you should also put an hour of your week reading news reports about your competitors.

## Build Relationships

In the process of learning about your industry, try to build relationships inside and outside of your organization. In your organization, make it a point to start making relationships with other leaders who are at least one level above you. Outside of the company, you could also take time to learn who the up and coming personalities are. It will serve you well to find opportunities to be in the same room with them to start relationships.

Effective leaders understand that important relationships take time to develop. You will not gain important relationships overnight. To build professional relationships, make it a habit to show genuine interest to the people you want to know more. Successful networkers show full engagement every time they are in a conversation with the people they want to connect with. For instance, they always maintain eye contact and they always have presence of mind while talking. They also try to avoid looking at their phones or looking around while talking to these people.

It is also a good habit to learn about the people behind the positions. Most people only want to talk about your work and your strategies. Instead of doing this, you could make it a point to learn about the life of the person. For example, ask about their families and their personal interests outside of work.

While interacting with people, also try to learn how they communicate. You may also observe verbal and non-verbal cues that the person uses to communicate. By learning these types of information from your connections, you will be able to read people more effectively. You will be able to gauge if the person is reliable or not. You will be able to identify the emotions that the person is trying to hold back.

Gaining the right types of connections gives you the ability to ask for favors in the future. While most of us want to avoid using these favors, there will come a time when you will need help. If you maintain a good relationship with the people around you, they will not hesitate to help you out if they can.

In the same way, also try to help the people around you if you can. When people ask for your help, you at least try to help that person. You should consider the amount of future value of that person for your career. At the very least, the favors that people owe you can be used to help you do your day-to-day task as a leader in your organization.

# Chapter 2 – Learn about Your Followers

Now that you know about the playing field where you will exert your leadership, you may start focusing on your followers. Generally, you want to know of the best way to use your human resources to reach the organization's goals.

## *Who are your followers?*

Are you an individual contributor?

You should start by identifying the types of people that you are leading. All people start out as individual contributors in the organization. While this usually includes the lowest level positions in the organizational chart, you can already start practicing your leadership skills from here. At this level, your goal is to lead yourself to improve your individual contributions to the organization. You could also start building your leadership reputation by being dependable.

Are you a manager?

If you are a manager of some sort in your company, chances are that you are leading a group of individual contributors. When you are given a managerial position, the company assumes that you are already an expert at being a contributor. Your goal is to translate your knowledge on how to improve individual performance towards your followers. You use your experience of being a contributor to help others become more productive and efficient in their job.

Are you a leader of leaders?

Eventually, you will get a position where you are leading other leaders. People in the human resources industry usually get this kind of job. Ideally, you should not take a position like this if you have no experience in being a manager/leader of individual contributors.

Are you an organizational leader?

If you progress further in your career, you will get a chance to be a leader that creates changes in companywide policies. When you get this kind of job, you are already leading entire functions and divisions. These posts are usually given to vice presidents of companies.

Are you the top leader of your organization?

Lastly, you could also be given the task to lead entire organizations. Presidents or CEOs of companies have this kind of role. This kind of leadership requires a different set of skills compared to lower level leaders.

To be this kind of leader, you should have a vision on what you want the organization to become. If the organization has reached its peak performance, this type of leader finds a way to reinvent the company so that it will be rejuvenated and it will continue to grow.

## *With great powers come great responsibilities*

As you rise in the ranks in your organization, the impact of your success in your leadership becomes greater and the scope of your decision-making increases. If you are a manager, your decisions only affect one branch of the company. However, as you improve to being a regional director, your decisions now affect multiple branches in a specific region.

The stakes of your decision-making also increases. If you make mistakes in making decisions, the amount of money lost and the business-related consequences are bigger if you are in the upper echelons of the company.

Lastly, people in higher positions of leadership in an organization are in charge of changes that create long-term effects in the organization. Vice presidents and CEOs are responsible for long-term changes that place the organization towards advantageous positions when competing in the future.

## *What do you want your followers to do?*

After identifying your followers, you should define what you want them to accomplish. In most cases, the goals are dictated by the organization. While the organization may give you the sales numbers or the project objectives, you could change it according to your knowledge of the capabilities of your followers.

Let's say the organization wants you to double your team's output in the following month. However, you are aware that your team has the potential to do better. You can motivate the team to do better than the goal required by the organization.

On the other hand, you may also lower the bar set for your team if you think that it is wise to do so. Let's say a college is pressuring its basketball team to become state champions. However, the coach knows that the feat is impossible at the current status of the team. Instead of aiming for gold, the coach just motivates the team to do their best and gain experience. They may reach for better outcomes when the players have gained the necessary experience.

The goals of the organization also vary depending on its current stage of development. An organization that just launched will require more work. However, there will be more milestones in these in startups compared to more established organizations. A leader in this type of organization will have fewer resources. However, the expectations are also considerably less.

A mature organization on the other hand, will require more management than strategic leadership. In an older organization, it may be more important to explore new markets, develop new products and reinvent company culture to rejuvenate the company.

# Chapter 3 – Put Yourself in your Followers' Shoes

To become an effective leader, you need to influence the people you lead to work for your goal. You want all the members of your organization to participate. At times, you will need to motivate people to keep doing the actions you prescribe even if they do not want to.

If you have ever tried leading people in the past, you know that the tasks discussed above are easier said than done. Many reasons come to mind as to why many people fail to be effective leaders. However, one of the recurring reasons always has something to do with the distance between the leader and his or her followers.

## Your followers are focused on their own goals

Most people think that they can be effective leaders if they just communicate the goal to their followers. However, they learn the hard way that it takes more than that to influence the behavior of other people. If you want to influence how other people act, you should first learn about them.

Most people are self-centered. They think of themselves as the protagonist in their own movie. They think that every other person is a side character that will help create their story. It is almost impossible to change this way of thinking.

Your followers have a similar way of thinking. They are always thinking based on their own self-interest. They do not care about the organization's goals. Most of them do not care of how hard you worked as a leader. Instead, they are more interested in working towards their own personal goals.

Your job as a leader is to find out about the goals of your followers. You need to learn about what they want in life. It could also be useful to learn about their top most priorities.

By learning about these things, you will be able to adjust your way of motivating your followers.

## Learn about your followers by putting yourself in their position

Most managers are too focused on the goals of their organization or their company that they do not think of how their followers feel. This usually leads to discontent among the followers and they end up ignoring the goals of the company.

It is common for discontented employees for example, to think that their company does not care about them. Those in the lower ranks of companies often think that the leadership has never experienced doing their jobs. Discontented employees often feel that they are treated like resources rather than human beings.

In most cases, the employees' feelings are justified. The policy makers in most big companies never experienced to be working eight hours of manual labor a day. As a result, their employees see them as bosses that need to be followed. They are not viewed as influential leaders.

Authoritative leadership only works for short-term projects. However, if you want to influence people in the long term, a better approach may be required. You need to learn about the people you are leading by putting yourself in their shoes.

If you want your followers to believe in you, you need to make them think that you care about their wellbeing. To effectively communicate to your followers that you understand them, try to see things from their perspective.

You can do this by learning about the little details of some of your followers' lives. For instance, on your lunch break, invite one of your followers to eat lunch with you. While eating, you could ask him or her about his personal life. Also ask them about where they live and how they get to work from their home. You may also ask about their family. By doing this, you instantly build rapport with your followers.

Some people will hesitate to open up to you. You can make them confess about their personal lives by giving away some details of your own personal life. Be prepared with stories that will suggest vulnerability. When your followers see you opening up, they may do the same.

When you are alone after lunch, you could try to imagine what it is like for that person to come in every day and do their tasks at work. This way, you will know about the motivations of other people.

## Make a habit of being interested in other people's lives

People like talking about themselves. You should not limit your curiosity to the people you lead. Instead, make it a habit to be interested in the lives of other people. This will allow you to learn about how different other people's lives are to yours. This will expose you to many sources of motivation that you can use in your leadership roles.

When meeting new people, you could think of questions to ask. While they talk, be attentive and actively listen to what they have to say. You can show this by looking them in the eyes when they talk and allowing them to finish before you start adding your own input. Avoid one-upping others.

Instead of giving suggestions or advice, train yourself to keep on asking questions when in a conversation. You never know what you can learn by asking about the experiences of other people.

By actively learning about the lives of other people, you create a deep connection with them. Most people will love you when they see your appreciation in their life and in their work. Because most people enjoy talking about themselves, they will enjoy talking to you and they will think that you are easy to talk to.

## Choose the people with whom you build relationships

As a leader, you will not have enough time to learn about all of your followers. Instead of eating lunch with all of your followers, choose only a handful to connect with. You can refer to this group of people as your 'mastermind group'. This group should be composed of followers who are competent enough to delegate work to.

By creating a mastermind group, you only need to create deep connections to a fewer number of people. You can delegate the important tasks to this group. This technique is perfect for introvert leaders. Introvert leaders feel drained after interacting with too many people.

# Chapter 4 – Aim to Make All Stakeholders Happy

Most types of leadership roles still need to deal with bosses or people with higher positions. We can refer to bosses as overseers because they oversee the job of the leaders.

For most business managers for example, the overseers are the CEO or other executives of the company. For most self-employed individuals, the overseers are the clients. Even CEOs need to deal with shareholders of the company and ensure that they are happy with the earnings of the company.

Most leadership roles are a balancing act between the wants and needs of the overseers and the wants and needs of the followers. The average employee for example, only cares about his or her pay at the end of the day. They may also care about the time that they get off work or the number of days that they can rest from work.

On the other hand, in a regular business, the usual overseers (executives and shareholders) want profits to rise. They want to maximize the amount of time and productivity that can be squeezed out from each employee. Most of the time, the conflict in the interests of the overseers and the followers is the big barrier in achieving the organization's success.

## Set lower expectations with overseers

Once you assume the leadership position, try to take control of the expectations of the overseers. When talking about profit projections to the shareholders for example, tell them that the company is facing a financially rough year. If you need to organize an event for the organization, try to emphasize the difficulties of organizing the event when you meet with the overseers.

## Over prepare for the task at hand

This does not mean however, that you could lower your goals or underperform. You still need to work hard even if you have successfully lowered the overseer's expectations. You still need to show them a plan on how you will achieve the goal that the organization wants. However, you should not allow the overseers to set impossible goals and targets. These types of targets and goals will be taxing for your followers. If the goals are too difficult, you may need to push your followers to a slave-like existence at work. This will make you less popular. It is better to set a lower standard to the higher ups.

## Deliver beyond the overseers' expectations

If you have successfully lowered the expectations of the overseers, the next step is to over-deliver on your promise. By doing so, you may gain rewards for reaching quotas or get productivity bonuses. You will satisfy the expectations of the overseers because they are lowered to manageable levels. You also improve your popularity among your followers because you have led them to success.

## Avoid taking leadership roles when expectations are too high

A leader who takes the reins of the company in a booming economy is doomed to fail. When the economy is booming, sales numbers are usually up. Profits sore to new heights, and so do quotas and expectations of overseers. It is almost impossible for new leaders to lower the expectations of the overseers at this point.

It will be harder for new leaders to take the leadership position at these times. When the 'bust' part of the boom-bust cycle starts, you will be blamed for the failure of the company to reach its goals even though the organization never had the chance to reach its goals to begin with. You will be the scapegoat of the company and the overseers to save face to the public and to their employees.

You may have your reputation damaged beyond the chance of recovery. People will see you as a failure. They will not consider that the odds were against you when you took the leadership role. They will only focus on your failure.

Instead, you should time your entry to the leadership positions at a time when the organization is down. When taking a coaching job for example, it is easier for good coach to build his or her reputation with a lower ranked team. If he takes control of a championship contender, any achievement below the championship goal will be considered a failure. If the coach takes a losing team, any finish better than the previous year's ranking will be considered a success.

This approach to leadership is best used if you are just starting out with your leadership career. It is better to lead and improve badly performing organizations to glory.

# Chapter 5 – Work on Improving Your Reputation

A leader with a larger than life reputation can influence people from the first day. If you are popular as a leader, your reputation will begin to precede you to your future followers. People will look forward to working with you. They will want to be your apprentice because you are considered an important person in your industry.

To build this kind of reputation, you need to plan your image and to start stacking up achievements.

**Keep your overseers happy**

It is important to keep your overseers happy and to keep your connections with them. Most people leave their jobs with a bad relationship with their former bosses. This is usually a bad move, career-wise.

When you are in a job or in a position in the company, try to keep the overseers happy. As you leave the company, it is better to keep the relationship with your overseer intact so that you can still ask for a referral from them. It is also beneficial to your career to avoid any conflict with them because you will still need them in the future.

In the same way, try to be mindful of the feelings of your overseers. Just like other people, bosses tend to be vain with their reputations. Even if you did all the work for a particular project, you must still acknowledge the participation of your bosses in the process. Try to give them credit for the advice they gave and their decision-making skills throughout the process.

If you take all the credit from your overseers, their egos may get hurt and this may work against you. If you do not give them even a little bit of credit, they may feel jealous of your achievements. Some of them may even feel insecure and feel that you are trying to take over their jobs.

You don't want this kind of relationship with your overseers. You want to keep them satisfied for as long as you are not ready to replace them.

## Keep your personal intentions hidden from both overseers and followers

Just like the company or the organization, you have your own personal goal that you want to achieve. You should keep these personal goals hidden from your bosses as well as your followers. When people know what you want to achieve, they have a better chance of manipulating you. They will easily connect your behavior towards you intentions. The smarter players in your organization will also be able to guess your next moves because they know what you want.

By keeping your intentions hidden from the people around you, you can be more unpredictable in your behavior. Let's say you want to become the CEO of your company someday. The current CEO will feel like you want to replace him on his post. Other people aspiring for the position will also sabotage your success to limit the number of competition for the spot.

If you keep your intentions hidden, you will be able to prepare for your goal without people getting in your way. You let people interested in the position fight over it while you stack up on resources for your campaign for your personal goal.

You can keep your intentions hidden from the people in your organization by not talking about it a lot. If you want to become president of the company for example, try to avoid talking about it to the people around you.

If you want to quit your job in the future to start your own business, keep your plans to yourself until you are ready to break away from the company. The information may reach your superiors and they may try to delay your success so that you will not leave the company.

Keep your intentions guarded in your mind. When doing small talk, some people may ask you about your personal goals. Be ready with a script in answering this question. Generally, it may be easier to tell these people what they want to hear so that they stop asking you questions.

To keep your intentions hidden, limit your reactions when talking about the things that you want. When talking to your boss for example, try to limit your reactions when he talks about promotions especially if you are not ready to pursue it. Instead, you should only show interest in it when you are in a position to grab it.

If you show your interests too early, the people who are trying to manipulate you may try to use it to control your behavior. Your bosses and your followers alike will try to do this. In the process, you will be acting towards their wants rather than towards your own personal goals.

## Establish the foundation of your leadership

All successful leaders have values and principles that become the foundation of their leadership. These qualities separate them from amateur leaders. From the beginning, think of the values and principles that you want to add to your brand of leadership.

Among them, you should make integrity as the base or the foundation of your style of leadership. If you act with integrity most of the time, your followers will think that they can trust you. They will not doubt that your suggestions and actions are for the betterment of the team.

Aside from integrity, also include productivity and hard work as a part of the values that you uphold. You may also include a winning attitude and a competitive spirit. You may also include the constant drive for self-improvement in the list.

It is up to you to choose the values that you want to include in your personal brand of leadership.

## Talk and act according to your chosen leadership traits

After choosing the values and principles that you want to become the foundation of your leadership, make them your guide in making decisions in your daily leadership activities.

If you think of integrity as the foundation of your leadership for example, you will not say or do anything dishonest. You will always choose the fair and honest choice when making decisions.

If you want your team to work hard, you must also embody that trait. Show them that you are an effective leader by working hard. Also, make it a habit to be the first to arrive in the office in the workday and be with the team when your leadership is most needed.

Leaders whose words are consistent with their actions are regarded as more credible and trustworthy by the employees. Studies show that this type of leader is more effective in improving employee morale, productivity and work engagement.

On the other hand, leaders that are seen as dishonest create an atmosphere of mistrust and cynicism in the organization. This leads to low morale a low performance from employees.

**Show your competitive spirit**

Only competitive people are fit to hold leadership positions. If you are not usually competitive, change your ways so that you create a reputation that you will fight for what you think is right. Overseers love to hire leaders that they know will fight for the goals of the company. Followers also love to follow competitive leaders because these types of leaders have a better chance of becoming successful.

Ideally, you should avoid competition in business whenever possible. This practice allows you to preserve your resources for the long haul. However, there are times when you just need to compete with other people or organizations. When you see yourself in such a position, be ready to face the challenge. You must learn to compete in reaching the organization's goals. By showing this characteristic to your followers, you are also creating the same competitive spirit among them.

By creating a sense of competition, you will give your followers a reason to keep on being persistent. You will awaken the urge to win among your followers. You will give them a reason to get up every morning and start working.

To show your competitive spirit, try to show persistence in action towards your goals. The best time to show your competitive spirit is when you or your organization is facing adversity. In tough economic times for example, most people would give up reaching sales quotas. A competitive leader on the other hand, will continue to look for ways to work towards success.

The leader may try to enter a new market. He or she may also use new technology to reach more people to sell to. Competitive spirit alone will not ensure that you will succeed in leading your organization. However, it goes a long way in motivating your followers to keep working hard for the goals of the organization.

## Keep yourself relevant in your circles

You will have no reputation to uphold if people forget about you. Effective leaders avoid this at all costs by keeping themselves relevant in their circles. Many people disdain the idea of being the center of attention. Try to embrace this role so that the people around you will always remember you.

You must become the center of attention in a subtle way. For instance, try to use your skills and your personal attributes that other people do not have. If you are conventionally good-looking for example, use it as an asset to gain attention. You could also use fashion to enhance the unique aspects of your looks.

## Protect your work and ideas from credit thieves

You should have your own accountability chart when you work. This is a chart showing your accomplishments for each workday. Make it a habit to report the tasks that you did for your company to your boss at the end of each day. By doing so, you prevent other people from taking credit of the work that you did.

The same level of diligence should be done when you are in a leadership position. Make sure that you protect the work of the people who follow you. You should ensure that credit is given to the right person. If credit translates to real life rewards, it is important to your followers that the people who deserve the rewards receive it.

By protecting the works and ideas of your group from being stolen, you improve your reputation among your followers. Your followers will think that you are trustworthy and they will share their ideas with you without fearing that you will take credit from it.

## If you can help it, avoid arguments

Arguments are often a waste of time. Leaders who argue too much do not get the job done.

Instead of being labeled as an argumentative person, create the reputation of being a man or woman of few words. Choose to be known as a person of action. Your actions should lead to your success.

Most people will create judgments when they observe you while you are arguing. Others will try to use your emotions against you. If you have the reputation of having a temper, people will use your frequent bursts of anger to cloud your judgment.

## Aim to act with emotional intelligence

When leading others, you will meet different type of personalities. Some of them are easy to work with. If you have a choice, you should look for people whose work habits blend well with yours.

In most cases, however, there is always someone in the group whose personality type will clash with yours. Misunderstandings always arise during stressful situations. At these times, effective leaders always act with emotional intelligence.

Emotional intelligence allows you to act objectively even in stressful situations. A person with an underdeveloped emotional intelligence is easily agitated. He becomes angry or emotional easily especially in pressurized situations.

To start developing your emotional intelligence, look back in your past behavior and check how you act during stressful situations. Try to identify the emotions that you project outward that may damage your relationships in the future.

After identifying your common emotional reactions, try to identify the triggers of these emotions. You should also identify your pet peeves so that you will be more prepared when you encounter them in the future.

If you successfully identify your triggers, start looking for solutions to these emotional reactions. Some people for instance, find it effective to step back from the stressful situation and think before making a decision.

After receiving negative news for example, most people choose to do the first reaction that comes into their minds. Some would cry while others would become angry.

The moment you experience an emotional trigger, that is the time when you are most vulnerable to emotional outbursts. Your goal during these stressful situations is to delay the emotional outburst so that the mind will have time to process the emotions and the situation behind it.

After delaying the emotional outburst, try to find ways to channel your emotions without being aggressive towards other people. Some leaders use exercise to release tension from their stressful days.

Some people also write on personal journals their thoughts and feelings about a situation. Others find it more effective to communicate to their confidants. You should find your own way to relieve stress.

## Control your emotions when interacting with your followers

Most authoritarian leaders use fear as a tactic to keep their followers in line. These types of leaders use anger and aggression as their primary way of dealing with stress.

While fear may work in some instances, it only works for short periods. When followers are in a constant state of fear, they tend to be more stressed. This constant feeling of stress drains their energy throughout the workday. They are no longer engaged in the work they are doing because they are only looking forward for each day to end. The energy level at the workplace decreases when the boss is not looking and productivity falls.

For a more sustainable approach, effective leaders choose to use a firm but nurturing approach towards their followers. In times of stress, they do not communicate with aggression. Instead, they begin each conversation with empathy. They use scripts like:

"I know this is not easy for you" or "I understand that you are having a hard time"

When pointing out changes that need to be made, an effective leader does not blame the others but tries to focus on the solution to the problem. Instead of blaming the organization or the employees, an effective leader focuses the conversation on the outcome that he or she wants and the solutions to reach that.

You should also do the same. By acting with emotional intelligence and controlling your emotion when dealing with followers, you are protecting your reputation as a leader. Leaders who are calm in the face of stress are the ones that are more successful in influencing their followers.

### Anger should be used strategically

There are times when showing anger and aggression is justified. In sports for example, team leaders usually show anger at the situation as a result of their passion for the game. Sometimes, showing anger and aggression as a sign of passions will motivate the team to do better.

However, you must only use it in selected situations. Before showing anger, attempt first to assess if it is truly the more strategic option. In addition, you must ensure that your anger or acts of frustration are not directed towards your own follower.

# Chapter 6 – Subtle Tricks to Influence People

As a leader, you want to become a master manipulator without the reputation of being one. When people think that you like to play mind games, they will be wary every time they are dealing with you.

Your influence towards others starts with how they see you as a person. You want people to like you. If they like you enough, they may give way to your requests and your suggestions.

You want your followers and your overseers to keep their guard down when dealing with you. You can do this by creating an impression of being dumber than you actually are. Most people are too vain to let others think that they are dumb.

## Don't get caught when studying people

Effective leaders do not show signs that they are studying other people. When observing key followers, be subtle. If possible, only observe your key followers when they have no way of seeing you. You could do this behind one-way mirrors or through cameras.

When observing other people, your goal is to find out what motivates them. With most people, you learn this information simply by looking at their social media accounts. Most people will show the source of their passions through their personal posts. A parent for example, posts mostly about their children. This may mean that they are working hard because they want their children to have a good life. You may be able to motivate this type of follower by giving rewards related to their parenting needs.

On the other hand, a person who is always posting about shopping on his or her social media account may love luxurious things. He or she may be easily motivated with material rewards.

## Use people's passions to motivate them

The best leaders adjust their methods of motivation based on the source of passion of the person they are motivating. Rewards for example, are the most common types of motivation used by leaders. However, rewards will only work for short-term goals. If you want to sustain your followers' motivated efforts, you want to align the goals of the company or organization to the goals of the goals of the person you are trying to motivate. If you are dealing with a family man for example, he may want to be promoted so that he can provide the future needs of his family. If you see evidence in your observation of that person that this is true, you must use this information to improve the person's performance in the team.

You can create a step-by-step plan to that person so that he will be promoted. In the plan, add tasks that you personally want him to accomplish. You could then tell that person that he would be considered for the promotion if he accomplishes the tasks in the action plan.

By doing the method above, you will be able to motivate the person to perform better. If you are considering more than one person for the promotion, you may let them know about it ahead of time. The person with the better skillset for the position should come out on top.

### Avoid giving criticisms

Many managers try to boost other people's performance by pointing out the mistakes they made. Unfortunately, these managers were never informed that most people do not respond well to criticisms. Instead of doing well, people tend to perform less effectively when they are criticized.

When trying to influence others, you will motivate others better if you avoid criticizing their work. Instead of criticizing, suggest alternatives to what they are doing. For instance, you may point out that when you were in their position, you made many mistakes. You could then elaborate the mistakes that you do not want them to repeat. By stating it this way, you never criticize them for their mistakes. Instead, you are telling them that you did the same mistakes in the past and that you were able to improve your performance by doing certain changes.

## Lower your followers' guard by being more relatable

Most people think that being a leader means that they should keep a perfect image. This is not always the case. If you are too perfect in the eyes of your followers, they may not follow your advice because you are not very relatable. People usually follow leaders that they see themselves in.

For instance, a group of students is more likely to follow a teacher closer to their age rather than someone significantly older. The younger teachers are more likely to see the situation from the students' eyes. This shared perspective allows the younger teacher to bridge the gap between the older teacher and the students.

If you are not relatable to the eyes of the people you are supposed to lead, it will be hard for you to motivate them to do what you want. They will not trust you and they will always be on guard when they are dealing with you. When their guard is up, they are less likely to heed suggestions and advice.

To be more relatable to the people you are leading, you must show signs that you are just like them. There are many ways to achieve this. For instance, you could choose special occasions to bond with your followers. When bonding with them, participate in their activities to be accepted by the group.

You could also do this by spending time with the people you lead on regular workdays. For instance, spend your lunchtime with them or invite some of the more influential member of the group for dinner. You could win that person over so that he or she will introduce you to the group.

In more extreme cases, you could lower the guards of your followers by showing a sign of vulnerability. For instance, try standing up for the group against your own boss. By doing so, you will be able to gain the trust of your followers. While this is effective in winning over the trust of your followers, it is also risky. Effective leaders only do this when they are certain that their overseer will not get rid of them for doing so. If you trust your overseer, you can also stage the misunderstanding just to gain the trust of your followers.

## Mirror the other person's actions

When talking with someone that you want to influence, use the mirroring technique to be liked by the other person. To use this technique, you first observe the little mannerisms of the person you are talking to. Some people for instance like to cross their legs in a certain way. Others have a compulsion to touch their hair when they are stressed.

You observe the little things that the person that you are talking to is doing. After few minutes, try to copy the gesture or mannerism. Also, make sure that the other person is looking at you when you do it.

When you mirror another person's gestures or actions, you are showing that you have similarities with that person. The person you are talking to will think of you as relatable and it increases the chance that they will follow what you are saying.

## Influence people based on their need to believe

Humans are created with the urge to believe. This is the reason why most people still follow religions even though there is no proof that supernatural beings exist. People are mentally hardwired to have a sense of belief in something they are passionate with.

One example of a need to believe is our urge to find a good leader to follow. Certain types of personalities prefer to follow than lead. If you just create an image of an ideal leader, you will be able to win over these personality types. This is the reason why big companies often change their CEO in rough economic time. The new leadership creates hope in the hearts of the workforce. The newfound hope is more likely to motivate them to keep themselves motivated.

Your timing in taking the leadership position is crucial if you want to create this type of effect among the people you lead. Steve Jobs for example, returned to

Apple when the Mac was struggling against other PC brands. His reentry to the leadership position created a hope among long-term Apple employees. This atmosphere also gave them the ability to hire new engineers for product development.

A good time to enter a leadership position is when the existing followers are discontented with the current leadership. If you enter the company or the organization at this time, even small achievements will be viewed by your followers as great wins for the group. This will motivate them even more to do better.

You may sustain the faith of your followers in you with timely wins for the organization. After winning a few small battles with your group, they will be confident enough to take on bigger challenges.

## Remove factors with negative effects to the group's motivation

As a leader, it is your job to make sure that the working environment is conducive to working. However, every now and then, you will encounter factors that may affect the motivation of your followers in a negative way. It is common for example, for you to find members of the group who are negative thinkers. When negative thinkers voice out their thoughts, they usually affect lessen the motivation of the people around them. Sometimes, people who are going through a rough phase in their lives may also create a sense of negativity in the group.

To prevent these members from affecting the motivation of the group in a negative way, getting rid of them is a good option. If possible, you could also fire people who tend to lessen the motivation of the group. If this is not possible, at least, limit their interactions with the other members of the group that you are leading.

# Chapter 7 – Motivating Followers for Long-term Tasks

Sustaining the motivation of followers is one of the greatest challenges for leaders. Studies show that humans are commonly motivated by three factors:

1. The need for safety and survival

2. The need to belong to a social group

3. The need to achieve one's full potential

In the workplace, people are most engaged in their tasks when they are working for the third need. The first and second needs are easily achieved. We usually stop working when these needs are satisfied.

The third need on the other hand requires a longer period or engagement. When people are working for this level of personal development, they are aiming for autonomy and mastery of their craft.

They also want to be contributing to something meaningful.

If you want your followers to be motivated for the long haul, you should make sure that they are working for this level of development. If you can successfully do this, you will see increased engagement among your followers.

Here are some tips on how to make your followers more engaged in the tasks that you want them to do:

**Make your followers think that they are recognized**

People become more excited to be a part of an organization if the leader makes them feel that they are recognized. The easiest way to do this is by knowing each follower by name. If you know a person's name, they are more likely to feel respected. This simple trick will make them like you. It makes them feel like a real part of the organization.

You can do this by giving each of your followers some tasks that are suited to their skills. Make sure to commend them if they do a good job.

Find ways to measure and recognize the effort that your followers put in. You can show your appreciation for them by thanking them personally for being engaged in the activities of the organization. You could also let them know how important their work is for the organization.

## Give your followers a task that fits their skills and interest

People become disengaged from their jobs when the tasks they are given do not match their interests and their skill level. If you give a talented a task that is too easy for him or her, he will easily get bored. They will just do the task fast to get it over with and start doing things that are more interesting to them.

Right from the hiring and recruitment stage, make sure that the people you hire have accurate expectations of the tasks that they are getting hired to do. They will be more likely to be engaged if they are aware of the company situation and the compensation package of the company from the beginning.

If the employees are paid less than they expect, they will feel disengaged from the goals of the organization.

## Provide constructive feedback, proper coaching and professional development opportunities

People often feel left out in an organization when they do not rise up in ranks. However, you cannot just give out promotions all the time to boost the morale of your followers. In between giving out promotions, aim to make your followers feel like they are growing inside the company. You can do this in three simple ways.

First, you could take the time to give constructive feedback to your followers. Instead of criticizing what they did wrong, focus on what they should do next time to improve. To make your criticisms constructive, create a system to measure the effort and results of your followers. Show them their performance numbers personally and give them tips on how to improve.

If possible, you must also create a system where in the newer members of the team get coaching from the more senior members. In some companies for example, people new to a position are given a week or two, shadowing a senior employee. This allows them to learn the practices of the organization from experience.

The best leaders always make sure that the coaches they assign have leadership characteristics as well. By delegating the coaching of newer organization members, you are also training the coaches to become future leaders.

Lastly, find opportunities for professional development for your followers. Most companies hold trainings for the certification of their employees. You should not stop there. You could also include special continuing education benefits for qualified members of the organization.

## Show your followers how they can grow inside of the organization

The talented members of your organization always have the option to leave the company for greener pastures. Disengagement is one of the first signs that a person is considering to leave a company.

To decrease the chances of this from happening, make sure that you show your followers how they can grow from within the organization. You can do this by showing them the career options from within the organization. You must influence them to reach for the top most spot before leaving the organization.

By influencing them to improve their ranks, they are more likely to become committed to staying in the organization.

## Create a working environment that allows regular rest periods

Find ways to encourage your followers to rest well in their breaks. Most people nowadays for example, spend their rest periods using social media. This type of activity still stimulates the senses. This is the reason why most employees still feel tired after 20-30 minutes of rest.

As a leader, you must ensure that your members do not feel overworked. You can do this by ensuring that they are getting the right amount of rest every day. If possible, the company should also limit the food available around the organization to healthy options. Healthier food options increase the energy levels of your followers improving their performance at work.

## Maintain the followers' trust towards organization leaders

People begin to feel disengaged when they do not trust their leaders. Aside from keeping your own image of integrity, build up the reputation of the senior leaders in your organization. By doing so, you give your followers someone to look up to. You could start by introducing them to your CEO. If the CEO of your organization has a good reputation, it will be easier to make your followers follow that person. On the other hand, if the organization has leaders with poor integrity, the followers will not take their words seriously. News and announcements from these leaders will be met with cynicism.

While you cannot control the reputation of other leaders, you can control the focus of your own followers. Instead of making them focus on the bad leaders of your organization, shift their attention to the ones who do have integrity. You should make the leaders with good reputations the representatives of your organization. This will boost morale of the followers because they think that their voices are being heard at the top.

# Conclusion

Thank you again for downloading this book!

I hope this book was able to help you to become a more effective leader.

The next step is to start building your leadership skills. The only way to learn the tips and tricks in this book is by using them daily. You could use this book as a guide when developing your influence and your leadership skills. Return to it regularly so that you will remember each lesson in it.

Over time, you will be able to integrate all these lessons in your leadership practices. These skills will help you reach the higher levels of your organization.

Thank you and good luck!

# Check Out Our Other Books!

Below you'll find some of our other books that are popular on Amazon and Kindle as well. Simply click on the links below to check them out. Alternatively, you can visit our publisher page on Amazon to see other work done by our other authors on our team.

Resume: The Secrets to Writing a Resume that is Guaranteed to Get You the Job

The Art of the Interview: The Perfect Answers to Every Interview Question

The Millionaire Real Estate Mogul: Strategies to Building Wealth with Real Estate

Sales: The Art of Selling: The Secrets that Top Sellers Don't Want You to Know

## About Increasing Sales, Income, and Profits

If the links do not work, for whatever reason, you can simply search for these titles on the Amazon website to find them.

## FREE MEMBERSHIP!

Congratulations! Lifestyle Initiative, Inc. Is giving you a free lifetime membership to one of it's premium arch teams.

What does this mean?

This means that you get to own Lifestyle Initiative's books before they go public in book stores all around the world. The only thing you will have to do is leave an honest review for these books and sign up to the link below.

This is a one-time offer and I am so excited to offer it to you today.

Please sign up now in the link below to receive free books similar to this and have your review make an impact on future products!

www.ingramcontent.com/pod-product-compliance
Lightning Source LLC
Chambersburg PA
CBHW061157180526
45170CB00002B/843